All Wind
and
Water

Cliff Hatton

Published by the Medlar Press Limited,
The Grange, Ellesmere, Shropshire.
www.medlarpress.com

ISBN 978-1-907110-07-8

Text and illustrations © 2010 Cliff Hatton

Design © The Medlar Press 2010

Cliff Hatton has asserted his right under the
Copyright, Design and Patents Act, 1988,
to be identified as Author and Illustrator of this work.

Designed and produced in England by
The Medlar Press Limited, Ellesmere.

All Wind and
and
Water

A Pike Fisher's Guide
to the Fens

Cliff Hatton

A Waterlog Book

2010

For the benefit of the
uninitiated, pictured here is
NOT proper drain-fishing.

Proper drain-fishing
is nowhere near
as exciting.

Drains' refers to a network of channels and ditches specifically designed to create viable farmland from waterlogged bogs and marshes. The best-known of these drain systems is that covering Cambridgeshire, Norfolk and Lincolnshire.

Construction started in 1626 when Dutch hydro-engineer, Cornelius Vermuyden, commandeered a group of enthusiasts to manually dig a twenty mile long trench thirty feet wide and ten feet deep.

In so doing, the Dutchman
disrupted the lives of thousands
of marsh-dwellers known as the 'Fen
Tigers' - thus committing an
act of mass genocide.

The Fen Tigers were a hardy breed renowned for their hunting and pike fishing skills.

For centuries it was believed that these people had adapted to their unique life-style by developing webbed feet!

But might there be a grain of truth in this seemingly outrageous idea?

Photographs recently
retrieved from beneath the
floorboards of an old
fisherman's hovel in
Flood's Ferry would appear
to substantiate those old beliefs.

It is unlikely that photographers
of late Edwardian period would
have possessed the skills necessary
to create convincing 'spoofs'.
So . . .

. . . might the gene live on?

More recent photographic
evidence suggests the gene's
survival has survived
into modern times.

Shown opposite is the Deputy
Mayor of Ely addressing
members of the Emneth
Turnip and Sugar-Beet
Enthusiasts in 1953.

Note the unusually
wide footwear of both sexes.

And here, an un-named
Three Holes housewife takes
advantage of a favourable
drying day, circa 1956.

Frustratingly, her feet are
obscured by the laundry basket
but might those socks provide
a clue? What would be the
point of such footwear if it was
not to provide the wearer
with a snug and
comfortable fit?

Surely this is positive proof
that webbed feet live on in the
wilds of East Anglia.

As is this - the 1959 annual
gathering of the Flatlands
Piscatorial Society.

(The publishers of this
book would be most grateful for
more information or photographic
evidence of webbed feet or other
unique and intriguing
biological data.)

Well, webbed feet or not,
the East Anglian Fens attract
pike anglers from all over the
country, helping to sustain
the hospitality trade and
the local economy.
Sales of whisky and
anti-depressants have more
than trebled since 1974.

Here, a pair of hopefuls prepare
for the long drive down
from the grandeur of the
Yorkshire Dales.

19

After a tough week at work
what could refresh the soul
as well as . . .

... a few days relaxation
beneath the vast open
skies of Fenland?

What better antidote could
there be to the monotony
of factory life . . .

. . . than the freedom of the fens?

For new-comers to Fenland
piking, there is always the
question 'Where do I start?'
Expert opinion is that
anglers should first
find a 'feature' . . .

. . . some bank-side cover
which Fenland fish, (bored out
of their brains) might perceive
as a point of interest.

Something like . . .

. . . a taller-than-average weed.

This is likely to flag-up
a real hot-spot . . .

. . . to be jealously guarded!

But a little diligence from a
keen-eyed piker should
eventually pay dividends.
This discarded 7-up
tin bodes well.

Once his baits are in the water,
he can sit back and relax
in the bosom of fenland
countryside at its
very best . . .

. . . far from the roar of traffic . . .

. . . and the bustle of city life.

Some more competitive
anglers are known to 'leap-frog'
older anglers. This will do
nothing to improve your
success with pike.

Proper 'leap-frogging'
however, is a method
which almost
guarantees a run . . .

. . . though many seasoned
Fenland pikers know that
float-fishing can often
provide the only sport
of the day!

At times, sport can be
very slow . . .

. . . like, very, very slow . . .

. . . but suddenly, all the rods
will 'go' at once!

a stroke, all the preparation
and waiting will seem
worthwhile . . .

. . . but invariably it's
just the drain being
pumped-off.

But this does give the
waterways a good 'flush-out' . . .

. . . and the opportunity
to try out new,
innovative methods.

And if there's just too much
water in the rivers, you could try
working hard at catching
in a local pond.

Fenland also attracts
visitors not as welcome as
anglers - such as
ferox ferox (or 'scumbags'
as they are fondly
known by locals).

Some people blame
the over-pilfering and
exploitation of their
natural hunting-grounds
for their erratic
behaviour . . .

But a study at the
Chakrabarti School of Sociology
concluded that the much-maligned
ferox ferox needs to steal
its own bodyweight in
electrical goods every day
in order to sustain his
way of life.

Ferox ferox are easily spooked whilst 'working'.

However, strange, mysterious ways prevail in the hinterlands of eastern England. Should you attempt to prevent a theft from your own house . . .

. . . its more than
likely it'll be you who
gets arrested!

But for anglers, Fenland
does have its nicer, friendlier side.
How about a little retail-therapy?
Look no further than the
Shippea Hill '8 'til late'!

Of course, government policies
are likely to affect fishermen
even in remote areas . . .

. . . but, in the main, pikers
visiting the region will still receive
a warm welcome - and find plenty
of interesting people to chat to.

If the piking is a bit slow,
why not try your hand
at shooting?

Or visit one of the region's
many ancient seats
of learning.

Marvel at the magnificent
ancient architecture . . .

. . . or take in the view from
one of Fenland's
breath-taking bridges.

Wild-life abounds . . .

You may even be lucky enough
to spot a legendary Fenland
thoroughbred horse.

You can jog down safe,
traffic-free lanes . . .

. . . lose yourself on mile after
mile of level,
dead-straight roads.

You can stroll through the leafy
canopies of Fenland.

And just a short walk will have
you at another 'hot' venue . . .

. . . raring to go . . .

. . . and eager to employ
new tactics.

There are even places where you

an fish two waters at once!

But anglers should be aware
of the 'Look-outs' - mysterious
Fenland characters who roam
the drains of East Anglia.

They spy on any incomers and
will sometimes go to enormous
lengths to satisfy
their curiosity.

Innocent anglers can
never be certain that they
aren't under surveillance and
a look-out could pop-up . . .

. . . at almost any time.

Today, retired look-outs live
quietly – often keeping fish
for a hobby.

But back to the fishing!
Newcomers to the fens might
well get their first glimpse of
a zander . . .

. . . and experience their delight
in the capture of a new and
handsome species.

But there's nothing quite like the thrill of taking up the slack and tightening into a formidable Fenland Esox . . .

. . . there to battle with the Master
of the Drain . . .

. . . or not, as the case may be.

ナナ

Fenland has been
enriched in recent times,
and not just with modern
angling methods.

Workers arrive
from all over the world,
eager to share in the wealth
of this upwardly-mobile
part of England.

Communication can be a problem,
but a common love of the
finer arts of fishing brings these
workers together as one
harmonious group . . .

. . . 'at one' with other
Brothers of the Angle.

But let's not forget
Cambridgeshire's old
stalwarts . . .

. . . experienced anglers, capable of
logically working out the answers
to fishy problems . . .

. . . weighing-up the pro's
and con's . . .

... before arriving at the
best decision.

And the great
joy of fishing
in the fens?

. . . you can always go home.

A Glossary of Useful Fenland Terms

Winter Visitor

Pole-fishing

'Drag'

Dabbler

Resident

Wader